W9-CLE-832

Staying Clean

by Robin Nelson

Series consultants: Sonja Green, MD, and
Distinguished Professor Emerita Ann Nolte, PhD,
Department of Health Sciences, Illinois State University

Pull Ahead Books

⌴ Lerner Publications Company • Minneapolis

Lerner Publications Company
A division of Lerner Publishing Group
241 First Avenue North
Minneapolis, MN 55401 USA

Website address: www.lernerbooks.com

Words in **bold type** are explained in a glossary on page 31.

Library of Congress Cataloging-in-Publication Data

Nelson, Robin, 1971–
    Staying clean / by Robin Nelson.
       p.   cm. – (Pull ahead books)
    Includes index.
    ISBN-13: 978–0–8225–2638–4 (lib. bdg. : alk. paper)
    ISBN-11: 0–8225–2638–7 (lib. bdg. : alk. paper)
    1. Hygiene–Juvenile literature. I. Title. II. Series.
RA780.N45 2006
613'.4–dc22   2004019653

Manufactured in the United States of America
1 2 3 4 5 6 – JR – 11 10 09 08 07 06

AH-CHOO! Sally covers her mouth when she sneezes. What should she do next?

Sally needs to wash her hands.
Staying clean helps keep us **healthy.**

Germs can spread when you sneeze. Washing your hands will help keep the germs from getting into your body.

Germs get on your hands when you sneeze. Then germs from your hands can get on toys you play with. Those germs can get on other people.

The germs can make other people sick. Keeping your hands clean helps everyone stay healthy.

When should you wash your hands?
Wash your hands before you eat.
Wash your hands after going to the
bathroom.

Wash your hands after playing outside. Wash your hands after touching animals.

Wash your hands when they look dirty. Make sure the other people in your family wash their hands too.

How do we wash our hands? Use
warm water and soap. Rub your **palms**
together to make lots of bubbles.

Rub the top of your hands. Rub between your fingers. Don't forget your nails and your wrists!

Rinse your hands with water. Dry your hands well with a towel. Germs love warm, wet places!

OUCH! Josh fell off his bike and scraped his knee. What should he do? Josh asks a grown-up to clean his knee and put a bandage on it.

It's important to keep cuts and scrapes clean. If dirt and germs get into a cut, it could become **infected**.

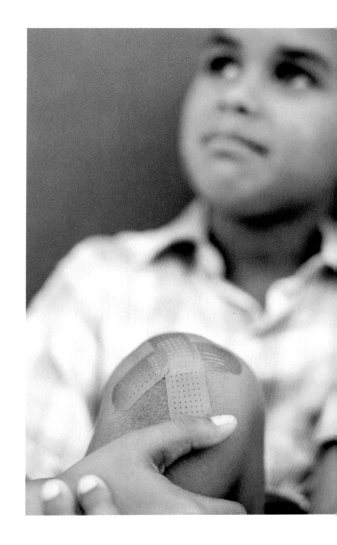

Rub-a-dub! Billy likes to take a bath.
Baths keep him clean and healthy too.
Baths and showers clean the germs
and dirt off our bodies.

Don't forget to wash your hair!
We need to keep our hair clean to
stay healthy.

PEE-EEW! You might start to smell bad if you forget to take a bath. Baths help us to smell good.

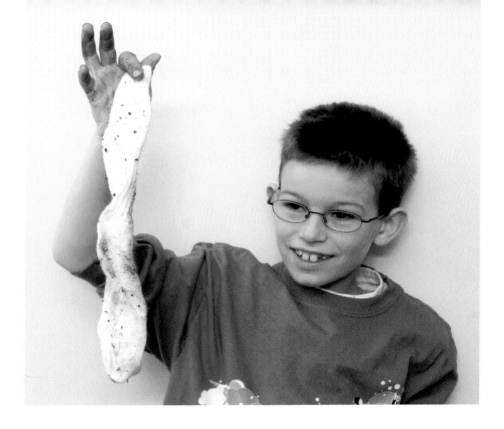

It's time to get dressed! Remember to
put on clean clothes. Dirty clothes
can start to smell bad. They are also
covered with germs.

Mike likes to wear a hat. He keeps his hat clean and does not share it with his friends. Germs and other tiny bugs called **lice** could get on his hat.

Lice make your head very itchy. They are also hard to get rid of. Never share hats, brushes, combs, or anything that touches your head!

Brushing our teeth keeps us healthy too.

Germs and food can get stuck on our teeth and make holes in them. These holes are called **cavities.** OUCH! Cavities can hurt!

Sarah brushes her teeth in the morning and before she goes to bed. She uses a little toothpaste and brushes gently.

She brushes her tongue too. This gets rid of germs and gives her good breath.

Staying clean makes us feel good. Washing hands, keeping cuts clean, taking baths, and brushing teeth help keep germs out of our bodies.

Doing all of these things helps keep us from getting sick. Staying clean keeps us healthy.

Let's Brush Our Teeth!

■ Molly brushes her teeth every day. She brushes them in the morning. She brushes them before she goes to bed. She brushes them after she eats.

■ Molly has a soft toothbrush. It's smaller than the one her older sister has. Molly's toothbrush is just the right size for her mouth and teeth. She will use her toothbrush for about three months. Then she'll get a new one.

■ Molly gets her toothbrush wet so its bristles are softer. She puts some toothpaste on her brush. Oops! She put too much on it. She needs only a small drop about the size of a pea.

■ Molly starts to brush her teeth. She moves her toothbrush in tiny circles on the front of her teeth and near her gums. She brushes the back of her teeth the same way. Next, Molly brushes the top of her teeth. She moves her toothbrush back and forth.

- Molly sings a song in her head as she brushes. That way, she knows she has brushed long enough. She needs to brush her teeth for about three minutes to get them clean.

- She brushes her tongue too! This will give her fresh breath. Brushing her tongue will also get rid of germs called bacteria. **Bacteria** can cause cavities.

- Finally, Molly uses **floss**. She moves the string up and down between her teeth and gums. Her dentist showed her how to do this. Flossing can help reach the food stuck between her teeth.

- Molly is done brushing her teeth. Have you brushed your teeth today?

Books and Websites

Books

Cole, Babette. *Dr. Dog.* New York: Knopf, 1997.

Mitchell, Melanie. *Killing Germs.* Minneapolis: Lerner Publications Company, 2006.

Moss, Miriam. *Scritch Scratch.* New York: Orchard Books, 2001.

Riccio, Nina. *Banish the Stinkies.* Canterbury, NH: Creative Attic, Inc., 1997.

Rice, Judith Anne. *Those Icky Sticky Smelly Cavity Causing But . . . Invisible Germs.* Saint Paul: Redleaf Press, 1997.

Swain, Gwenyth. *Wash Up!* Minneapolis: First Avenue Editions, 2002.

Thomas, Pat. *My Amazing Body: A First Look at Health and Fitness.* Hauppauge, NY: Barron's Educational Series, 2002.

Websites

BBC Health: Kids' Health
http://www.bbc.co.uk/health/kids/

KidsHealth.org
http://www.kidshealth.org/kid/

Glossary

bacteria: germs that can cause cavities, sore throats, and earaches

cavities: soft places or holes in your teeth that are caused by germs

floss: thin string that is used to clean between your teeth

germs: tiny living things that can make people sick

healthy: fit and well

infected: invaded by germs

lice: tiny bugs that can get in your hair and make your head itch

palms: the flat part on the underside of your hands

Index

Photo Acknowledgments

The photographs in this book appear courtesy of: © White Packert/The Image Bank/Getty Creative, front cover; © Todd Strand/Independent Picture Service, pp. 3, 4, 8, 10, 18, 19, 23, 24, 25; © Image Source/SuperStock, pp. 5, 7, 15; © The Photo Works/Photo Researchers, Inc., p. 6; © Tom Myers, p. 9; © Beth Johnson/Independent Picture Service, p. 11; © Royalty-Free/CORBIS, p. 12; © Brendan Curran/Independent Picture Service, p. 13; © Francisco Cruz/SuperStock, p. 14; Digital Vision Royalty Free, pp. 16, 22, 26, 29; © Darama/CORBIS, p. 17; BananaStock Royalty Free, p. 20; © Sam Lund/Independent Picture Service, p. 21; PhotoDisc Royalty Free by Getty Images, p. 27.